REVISE BTEC TECH AWARD
Enterprise

PRACTICE ASSESSMENTS Plus⁺

Series Consultant: Harry Smith
Author: Steve Jakubowski

A note from the publisher

These practice assessments are designed to complement your revision and to help prepare you for the external assessment. They do not include all the content and skills needed for the complete course and have been written to help you practise what you have learned. They may not be representative of a real assessment.

While the publishers have made every attempt to ensure that advice on the qualification and its assessment is accurate, the official specification and associated assessment guidance materials are the only authoritative source of information and should always be referred to for definitive guidance.

This qualification is reviewed on a regular basis and may be updated in the future. Any such updates that affect the content of this book will be outlined at **www.pearsonfe.co.uk/BTECchanges**.

For the full range of Pearson revision titles across KS2, KS3, GCSE, Functional Skills, AS/A Level and BTEC, visit:
www.pearsonschools.co.uk/revise

Published by Pearson Education Limited, 80 Strand, London, WC2R 0RL.

www.pearsonschoolsandfecolleges.co.uk

Copies of official specifications for all Pearson qualifications may be found on the website: qualifications.pearson.com

Text and illustrations © Pearson Education Ltd 2020

Produced, typeset and illustrated by QBS Learning

Cover illustration by Eoin Coveney

The right of Steve Jakubowski to be identified as author of this work has been asserted by him in accordance with the Copyright, Designs and Patents Act 1988.

First published 2020

23 22 21 20

10 9 8 7 6 5 4 3 2 1

British Library Cataloguing in Publication Data

A catalogue record for this book is available from the British Library

ISBN 9781292341781

Printed in Slovakia by Neografia

Acknowledgements

Getty Images: Richard Maschmeyer/Design Pics 14; **Pixabay:** Cristian Ibarra 1; **Shutterstock:** Alexey Lysenko 28, LightField Studios 42.

Notes from the publisher

1. While the publishers have made every attempt to ensure that advice on the qualification and its assessment is accurate, the official specification and associated assessment guidance materials are the only authoritative source of information and should always be referred to for definitive guidance.

Pearson examiners have not contributed to any sections in this resource relevant to examination papers for which they have responsibility.

2. Pearson has robust editorial processes, including answer and fact checks, to ensure the accuracy of the content in this publication, and every effort is made to ensure this publication is free of errors. We are, however, only human, and occasionally errors do occur. Pearson is not liable for any misunderstandings that arise as a result of errors in this publication, but it is our priority to ensure that the content is accurate. If you spot an error, please do contact us at resourcescorrections@pearson.com so we can make sure it is corrected.

Websites

Pearson Education Limited is not responsible for the content of any external internet sites. It is essential for tutors to preview each website before using it in class so as to ensure that the URL is still accurate, relevant and appropriate. We suggest that tutors bookmark useful websites and consider enabling students to access them through the school/college intranet.

Introduction

This book has been designed to help you to practise the skills you may need for the external assessment of BTEC Tech Award Enterprise Component 3: Promotion and Finance for Enterprise.

About the practice assessments

The book contains four practice assessments for the component. Unlike your actual assessment, the questions have targeted hints, guidance and support in the margin to help you understand how to tackle them.

 **Revision Guide** *page XX* links to relevant pages in the Pearson Revise BTEC Tech Award Enterprise Component 3 Revision Guide so you can revise the essential content. This will also help you to understand how the essential content is applied to different contexts when assessed.

 Hint to get you started and remind you of the skills or knowledge you need to apply.

 Prepare to help you on how to approach a question, such as making a brief plan.

 LEARN IT! to provide content that you need to learn such as a definition, rule or formula.

 Watch out! to help you avoid common pitfalls.

 Explore to remind you of content related to the question to aid your revision on that topic.

 Time it! for use with the final practice assessment to help you become familiar with answering in a given time and ways to think about allocating time for different kinds of questions.

There is space for you to write your answers to the questions within this book. However, if you require more space to complete your answers, you may want to use separate paper.

There is also an answer section at the back of the book, so you can check your answers for each practice assessment.

Check the Pearson website

For overarching guidance on the official assessment outcomes and key terms used in your assessment, please refer to the specification on the Pearson website. Check also whether you must have a calculator in your assessment.

The practice questions, support and answers in this book are provided to help you to revise the essential content in the specification, along with ways of applying your skills. The details of your actual assessment may change, so always make sure you are up to date on its format and requirements by asking your tutor or checking the Pearson website for the most up-to-date Sample Assessment Material, Mark Schemes and any past papers.

Contents

Practice assessment 1   1

Practice assessment 2   14

Practice assessment 3   28

Practice assessment 4   42

Answers   56

A small bit of small print

Pearson publishes Sample Assessment Material and the specification on its website. This is the official content and this book should be used in conjunction with it. The questions have been written to help you test your knowledge and skills. Remember: the real assessment may not look like this.

Practice assessment 1

Revision Guide
pages 52–53

Answer ALL questions.
Write your answers in the spaces provided.

Some activities in this paper must be answered with a cross in a box ☒. If you change your mind about an answer, put a line through the box ☒ and then put a cross in another box ☒.

The activities in this paper are based on this scenario.
You should read this scenario carefully before you start the activities.
Complete all the activities.

Scenario

Sam is passionate about protecting the environment. She volunteers for a national organisation that aims to reduce the impact of climate change. Sam has completed a design technology course and has used her skills to create a board game. There are two versions – one for children and one for adults. The game introduces the effects of climate change and suggests actions to reduce its impact.

The organisation where Sam volunteers is keen to support the development of her new board game. It has given her a grant of £10 000. Sam has excellent design skills but feels that she lacks the business knowledge to bring her board game successfully to the market. Sam has asked for your help on the financial and promotional aspects of her business, which she has called *Climate Solutions*.

Prepare

When reading through a scenario, using the initial letters of the word **CUBE** is a helpful way of collecting your thoughts together:

Circle the command verb.
Underline key information in the question.
Box key information in the case study.
Ensure you read each question at least twice before answering.

Hint

You will use the information in this scenario to help you answer the questions on pages 2–13.

Prepare

The questions that follow will require you to show your understanding of business, as well as to complete some calculations on aspects such as financial statements, cash flow and break-even analysis.

Revision Guide
page 14

Hint

'Complete' means drawing arrows to match each financial document to its purpose. Use a ruler so it is clear which boxes your arrow connects.

Watch out!

Read each box carefully before completing the diagram so you are clear on the purpose of each financial document.

LEARN IT!

You need to know the order in which sales and purchasing documents are processed. For example, when a business purchases goods from a supplier the first stage is to complete a purchase order.

Explore

It is a **legal requirement** to record accurate information in sales and purchasing documentation. This information is also used to prepare the main financial statements of the business, including the statement of comprehensive income and the statement of financial position.

Activity 1

Each month, Sam has to send her financial records to the national organisation. To ensure that the business's financial record-keeping is up to date and the financial documents are easily accessible, your first task is to start a filing system.

1 (a) Complete the diagram by drawing arrows to match each financial document with its use. An example has been completed for you.

Financial document	Purpose
Credit note	Sent to a supplier by the customer, this lists the products required from the supplier
Statement of account	Issued by the supplier to the customer so that money owed to the customer can be used to purchase goods at a later date
Purchase order	Sent by the supplier to the customer as acknowledgement that the order has been received
Delivery note	Sent to a customer by a supplier showing a summary of goods supplied and payments received

3 marks

Revision Guide
page 17

Sam asks you to check over an invoice she will be sending to one of her customers. She wants you to make sure that it is correct.

Climate Solutions

Date: 24 January 2020
Invoice: 73564/98

To: The Game Store
Tylers Hill
Grenlingham
GR4 V68

Please send payment to ....

Climate Solutions
London
BG4 7GF

Description	Quantity	Unit Price	Total price
Climate Solutions board game (Children)	8	£20.00	£160.00
Climate Solutions board game (Adults)	6	£25.00	£150.00
Score cards	14	£5.00	£70.00
		Sub total	£380.00
		Tax (VAT)	£76.00
Thank you for your business		**Total payable**	£456.00

Hint

Invoices show the names of the supplier and the customer. Read the document and the question carefully to make sure you identify the businesses correctly.

Watch out!

The amount payable on the invoice is the subtotal **minus** any discounts, **plus** any postage payable, **plus** VAT (calculated by finding 20% of the subtotal). In this invoice there are no discounts or postage costs, but they may apply in other scenarios.

(b) (i) State the name of the customer.

....

1 mark

(ii) Identify the total of the invoice before VAT is added.

£ ....

1 mark

Hint

'Identify' and 'state' mean you need to read the document carefully and select the correct piece of information. Simply give the answer.

(iii) Identify how much is owed by the customer according to this invoice.

£ ....

1 mark

Hint

'Explain' means you have to make a statement and then expand on its meaning.

(c) Explain the impact on Sam's business if the supplier doesn't pay the invoice on time.

....

....

....

....

2 marks

Watch out!

Read all the information thoroughly to ensure you understand it and can find the correct information.

Total for Activity 1 = 8 marks

Revision Guide
page 16

Watch out!

Read the additional information carefully because it contains important points. In this case you need to identify the **cost of postage and packaging** as it varies with the value of the order. In some questions discounts will vary according to the value of the order.

LEARN IT!

To calculate a percentage of a number, you must change the percentage to a decimal. For example, to calculate VAT you need to find 20% of the subtotal. So, you should multiply the subtotal by 20/100 or 0.2. This calculates the amount of VAT you need to add.

Hint

'State' means you need to provide brief, precise answers that use correct terminology from the specification. No further explanation is needed.

Activity 2

Sam has prepared a purchase order for supplies from *Craft Designs Ltd, Upton Industrial Estate, Devon, DV1 7HG*. Postage and packaging is free on all orders over £100. All other orders cost £15 for postage and packaging. Sam has asked you to complete the purchase order.

2 (a) Complete the order by filling in the shaded boxes.

Qty (cases)	Item description	Order code	Case size	Price per case £	Price per case p	Total price £	Total price p
3	Cardboard boxes	CB/1/B	5 per case	6	00	18	00
2	Varnish (1 litre tins)	V/1/A	2 per case	12	00	24	00
3	Paint brushes (4 cm)	PB/4/B	4 per case	20	00	60	00
2	Tape rolls	TR/10/C	10 per case	6	50	13	00
					Subtotal	(i)	
				(Postage and packaging)		(ii)	
				VAT @ 20%		(iii)	
				Total to pay		(iv)	

4 marks

Sam has asked you to help identify the potential market for the *Climate Solutions* board game.

(b) State **two** ways a market can be segmented.

1 ....

....

2 ....

....

2 marks

Total for Activity 2 = 6 marks

Activity 3

Sam has asked you to calculate some of the costs of the business.

3 (a) (i) Using the following financial information, calculate the total variable costs of producing 75 children's board games.

Variable costs for each board game produced
£4

Show your working.

Total variable costs of producing 75 board games = £ ....

1 mark

(ii) If the fixed costs of producing 75 board games is £1500, calculate the total costs of producing 75 board games.

Show your working.

Total costs of producing 75 board games = £ ....

1 mark

Sam is considering using direct marketing to promote sales of the *Climate Solutions* board game.

(b) Explain **two** benefits of direct marketing for Sam's business.

1 ....

....

....

....

2 ....

....

....

....

4 marks

Total for Activity 3 = 6 marks

Revision Guide
page 22

Watch out!

Show all your workings – in some cases you may gain marks even if your actual answer is incorrect.

LEARN IT!

To work out the **total variable cost**, identify the number of products and multiply by the variable cost per product.

LEARN IT!

Fixed costs remain the same however many products are made or sold. **Variable costs** depend on the number of products made or sold.

Hint

For each **benefit** you need to give a point and a short explanation. Use joining words or phrases such as 'therefore' or 'as a result' to help you.

Watch out!

Don't pick benefits that are too similar. Think of factors relating to increasing sales and improving branding, and say how these will be good for the business.

Revision Guide
pages 43–45

Hint

The equation identifies three values – **fixed costs**, **selling price** and **variable cost per unit**. Read the scenario and underline each of these values. Insert the correct values into the formula.

Hint

The variable cost 'per unit' means the same as 'per board game'.

LEARN IT!

Break-even analysis shows how many products a business needs to sell before it makes a profit. At the break-even point, total costs equal sales revenue. Any sales after this generate a profit.

Prepare

Practise sketching and labelling a break-even chart. This will help you remember the names of the lines.

Hint

You need to fill in the boxes on the chart with the correct labels. Look at the lines carefully. Remember, the total cost line represents the value of the fixed cost **and** the variable cost when added together.

Activity 4

Sam wants to know the number of board games (adult's version) that the business needs to sell to break even. You complete some research into the business costs. You find out the fixed and variable costs.

Fixed costs   £3250

Variable costs   £3.75 per board game

The selling price of the adult's version of the board game is £20.

The formula to calculate the break-even point is:

$$\frac{\text{fixed costs}}{\text{selling price per unit} - \text{variable cost per unit}}$$

4 (a) Calculate how many adult's board games the business needs to sell to break even.

> Show your working.
>
>
>
>   Number of board games to break even = ...

2 marks

Sam asks you to calculate the break-even point for the adult's board game. You decide to present the information to her in the form of a break-even chart.

(b) Label lines **A**, **B** and **C** on the break-even chart.

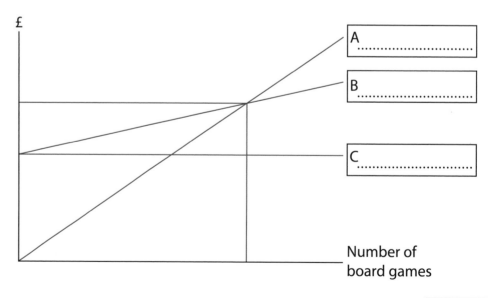

£

A ....

B ....

C ....

Number of board games

3 marks

Sam's promotional activities will include a public relations campaign.

(c) Explain **one** benefit to the business of using a public relations campaign to promote the *Climate Solutions* board game.

....

....

....

....

....

....

3 marks

As well as selling board games directly to the public, Sam will also supply business customers. These include toy shops and department stores. Business customers will benefit from 30 days' trade credit on each order.

(d) Explain **one** benefit of trade credit to Sam's business customers.

....

....

....

....

2 marks

Total for Activity 4 = 10 marks

LEARN IT!

Public relations includes press releases, exhibitions and sponsorship. You need to be able to explain the purpose and features of these public relations activities.

Watch out!

Look for the words in bold. Here you are asked to give **one** benefit and explain it. Make sure your answer only covers this. Don't answer with a list of benefits.

Hint

If a business buys on credit, payment for the order is deferred for a period of time, in this case 30 days.

Hint

For question 4(d), think about cash flow. A business may not be able to pay its suppliers until it has generated cash from its sales.

Revision Guide
pages 39, 40, 41

Hint

Give precise answers using correct terminology from the specification. A business generates cash from sales and spends cash on its suppliers.

Hint

An empty table will not get any marks, so fill in as much as you can.

Hint

Remember when completing a cash flow forecast, the closing balance from one month is the opening balance of the following month.

Hint

Underline key words in the additional information – **negative cash flow** and **net current assets**. You need to explain the relationship between these terms.

LEARN IT!

Net current assets is the **difference** between current assets (inventory, trade receivables, bank balance, cash on the premises) and current liabilities (trade payables, overdraft). The formula is:

net current assets = current assets – current liabilities

Activity 5

Sam has been advised to prepare a cash flow forecast. She asks for your help to draw together information about the business's cash inflows and outflows.

5 (a) State what is meant by a 'cash outflow'.

....

1 mark

(b) Complete the cash flow forecast for the first three months of trading.

	January £	February £	March £
Cash inflows			
Board games (children's version)	3250	3950	4000
Board games (adult's version)	1450	1650	2225
Total inflows	**4700**	(i).............	**6225**
Cash outflows			
Salary	2500	2500	2500
Purchase of equipment	1250	2575	0
Other costs	450	1825	2250
Total outflow	4200	6900	4750
Net cash flow	**500**	(ii).................	**1475**
Opening balance	300	800	−500
Closing balance	**800**	**−500**	(iii)...............

3 marks

Sam is concerned about the impact of negative cash flow on the net current assets of her business.

(c) Explain **two** reasons why net current assets are important to Sam's business.

1 ....

....

....

2 ....

....

....

4 marks

Total marks for Activity 5 = 8 marks

Activity 6

Sam wants you to calculate the profit made by her business after the first six months of trading. She asks you to explain what is meant by gross profit and net profit.

6 (a) State the meaning of the term 'gross profit'.

....

....

[1 mark]

(b) State the meaning of the term 'net profit'.

....

....

[1 mark]

Sam now wants you to complete the statement of comprehensive income. She can use this to identify the gross and net profit of her business.

(c) Fill in the shaded boxes to complete the statement of comprehensive income.

Statement of comprehensive income – *Climate Solutions* (projected figures for the first six months of trading)		
	£	£
Sales revenue (cash sales)		16 750
Sales revenue (credit sales)		(i)........................
Total sales revenue		30 000
Cost of sales		17 850
Gross profit		(ii)........................
Expenses		
Rent	2000	
Promotional leaflets	500	
Telephone	550	
Stationery	800	
Electricity	650	
Total expenses	(iii)...............	
Net profit		(iv)........................

[4 marks]

Revision Guide pages 24, 25, 29

Hint

Answer these questions by stating the formula for **gross profit** and the formula for **net profit**.

Prepare

Practise completing statements of comprehensive income, so you can do the calculations correctly.

Hint

Total sales revenue is made up of cash sales and credit sales added together.

Watch out!

Remember to **subtract** expenses and costs in the statement of comprehensive income. Calculating net and gross profit involves subtracting costs or expenses.

LEARN IT!

Money owed by customers who have bought on credit is not recorded in the statement of comprehensive income but is recorded as a current asset in the statement of financial position.

Revision Guide
pages 34, 35

Hint

You will be given formulas to calculate gross profit margin and net profit margin. Make sure you use the correct figures from the statement of comprehensive income and put them into the correct formula.

Hint

You will need to use gross profit and net profit figures from your answers to question 6(c).

LEARN IT!

Profit margins measure the amount of profit generated from each £1 of sales revenue. They are usually expressed as a percentage, so always include a % sign.

Hint

Profit is affected by costs **and** revenue. These factors can increase or decrease the level of profit. Choose one of these factors and explain the impact on profit if the figure improves.

You decide to use the figures in the statement of comprehensive income to calculate the business's profit margins. You will use the following formulas:

$$\text{gross profit margin} = \frac{\text{gross profit}}{\text{sales revenue}} \times 100$$

$$\text{net profit margin} = \frac{\text{net profit}}{\text{sales revenue}} \times 100$$

(d) (i) Calculate the gross profit margin of *Climate Solutions*.

Show your working.

Gross profit margin = ...%

1 mark

(ii) Calculate the net profit margin of *Climate Solutions*.

Show your working.

Net profit margin = ...%

1 mark

Sam asks you to look at the statement of comprehensive income and suggest actions that she could take to improve the net profit margin.

(e) Explain **one** action that Sam could take to improve the net profit margin of her business.

....

....

....

....

2 marks

Total for Activity 6 = 10 marks

Activity 7

Sam is thinking about future business plans, including a more expensive deluxe version of *Climate Solutions*. She will need new production machinery. Sam is considering leasing the new production machinery.

7 (a) Explain **one** advantage to *Climate Solutions* of leasing the new production machinery.

....

....

....

....

2 marks

(b) Explain two demographic characteristics in Sam's target market which could influence sales of the new deluxe version of *Climate Solutions*.

1 ....

....

....

....

2 ....

....

....

....

4 marks

Revision Guide
pages 7, 11, 51.

Hint

Purchasing equipment is expensive. Sometimes leasing equipment is better for the business.

Hint

The deluxe *Climate Solutions* is more expensive than the standard product. Think about the characteristics of consumers who might purchase the more expensive version. Demographic characteristics include **income, education and occupation**.

Revision Guide
pages 7, 11, 51.

Hint

'Evaluate' means you must explain the advantages and disadvantages of the two methods and come to a conclusion about the best method. You must justify your conclusion.

Hint

Your answer must focus on the business in the scenario – Sam's board game enterprise.

Hint

When considering the costs and benefits of a method of promotion, you must be clear about what the business is trying to achieve by promoting its products.

The launch of the new deluxe version of *Climate Solutions* will involve a range of promotional activities. Sam thinks she needs to appoint a sales team to do personal selling.

(c) Evaluate **two** methods of personal selling.

In your answer you should include:

- the key advantages and disadvantages of each method as a way of promoting *Climate Solutions*

- a conclusion which recommends the best method of personal selling for the *Climate Solutions* board game.

....

....

....

....

....

....

....

....

....

....

....

....

....

....

....

....

....

....

(c) Evaluate **two** methods of personal selling.

....

....

....

....

....

....

....

....

....

....

....

....

....

....

....

....

....

....

....

....

....

....

....

....

....

....

Hint

Justify your recommendation by making **linked points** – explain the benefits of your recommendation and the impact it will have on the enterprise's sales, revenue or profits.

Hint

When you have finished, re-read the question and make sure you have covered all the required points. Then check your spelling, punctuation and grammar.

6 marks

Total for Activity 7 = 12 marks

TOTAL FOR PAPER = 60 MARKS

Revision Guide
page 52

Practice assessment 2

Answer ALL questions.
Write your answers in the spaces provided.

Some activities in this paper must be answered with a cross in a box ☒. If you change your mind about an answer, put a line through the box ☒ and then put a cross in another box ☒.

The activities in this paper are based on this scenario.
You should read this scenario carefully before you start the activities.
Complete all the activities.

Scenario

Sunita is the owner of *Nature's Jewellery*. This enterprise uses sustainable materials to make Asian jewellery products aimed at young adults. Sunita is keen to expand her product range by making jewellery out of recycled materials. She needs business finance to purchase new equipment. She also wants to establish links with new suppliers and develop a promotional campaign for the launch of the new product range. Sunita must keep her business costs and revenue under review to ensure that the business generates a profit from sales of the new products.

Sunita currently runs the business on her own but thinks she will need additional help if her business plan is to be successful. She has appointed you as her Finance and Promotions Assistant to support the expansion programme.

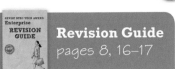

Activity 1

In your first meeting with Sunita, she explains that her main priorities are to promote the business and deal with the financial paperwork.

1 (a) Identify which of the following is an example of a public relations promotion.

☐ A   Junk mail

☐ B   Press release

☐ C   Buy-one-get-one-free

☐ D   Telemarketing

(b) Identify which of the financial documents in the boxes you would use to extract information regarding *Nature's Jewellery*'s costs, revenue and inventory. Insert a word from the list in each of the blank boxes:

- costs
- revenue
- inventory

Financial document		Purpose
Delivery note	→	(i) ....
Purchase order	→	(ii) ....
Customer invoice	→	(iii) ....

3 marks

Revision Guide
pages 3, 17

(c) Explain why Sunita should check the accuracy of an invoice before it is sent to one of her customers.

....

....

....

....

2 marks

(d) Give **one** example of an advertising method.

....

....

1 mark

Total for Activity 1 = 7 marks

Activity 2

2 (a) Fill in the shaded boxes to complete the following statement of account, which will be sent to one of Sunita's customers.

Statement of Account

Fashion Accessories   Date: 14 September
Keynsham   **Account number: 34786524**
Bristol
BR5 7HJ

Please send payment to:
Nature's Jewellery
Unit 8
Coptham Industrial Estate
Northfield
NR8 5RG

Date	Reference no.	Description	Amount (£)	Balance owing (£)
01.2.20	004537	Sale	375	375
05.2.20	008765	Sale	225	(i) ....
11.2.20	345298	Payment	(ii)	150
18.2.20	383765	Sale	200	350
23.2.20	338987	Sale	150	(iii) ....
25.2.20	373897	Sale	(vi)	700
27.2.20	986751	Credit	150	550
		Total due		550

4 marks

Sunita currently allows customers to pay for jewellery in cash or by credit card. She is considering accepting online payments.

(b) Give **one** reason why Sunita allows her customers to pay by credit card.

....

....

1 mark

(c) Give **one** disadvantage to Sunita of accepting cash payments from her customers.

....

....

1 mark

Total for Activity 2 = 6 marks

Revision Guide
pages 22, 26

Hint

Always read the extra information in the question. Use this to guide your answer so that you don't go off topic.

Hint

For question 3(a), you need to make two different points. Use related justifications to explain how each point affects the outcome for the business.

LEARN IT!

Reducing the cost of the materials will have a positive impact on overall profit. Increasing sales will also have a positive impact on profit.

Hint

Question 3(b) requires two distinct answers, as indicated by the numbering.

LEARN IT!

Assets are owned by the business, and appear on the statement of financial position. Current assets include stock. Fixed assets include vehicles and equipment.

Activity 3

Sunita has prioritised three areas that she thinks will improve the performance of her business:

1   Reducing costs
2   Increasing income
3   Improving efficiency

3   (a) Explain **two** ways in which Sunita could reduce the cost of the materials she uses to make her jewellery.

1 ....

....

....

....

2 ....

....

....

....

4 marks

(b) Explain **two** ways in which the sale of assets could contribute towards Sunita's business priorities.

1 ....

....

....

....

2 ....

....

....

....

4 marks

Total for Activity 3 = 8 marks

Activity 4

Nature's Jewellery made a profit of £4000 in its second year of trading, with an inventory of £2500 at the end of the year and a cash balance of £1000. Sunita has entered some of the figures into the statement of financial position for the second year of trading and has asked you to complete it.

4 (a) Complete the statement of financial position by inserting the correct figures from the scenario into the shaded boxes.

Statement of financial position – end of year 2		
	£	**£**
Assets		
Fixed assets	3000	
Current assets (comprising inventory and cash balance)	(i)........................	
Total assets		6500
Liabilities		
Current liabilities	1500	
Total liabilities		**1500**
Net current assets		(ii).....................
Net assets		(iii).....................
Owner's funds		
Owner's capital	(iv)........................	
Profit	**4000**	
		5000

4 marks

Hint

Read the additional information carefully. It has the figures for inventory, cash and profit. You need this information to calculate the values in the statement of financial position.

Hint

Double-check your answers to ensure you have put the correct figures in the right spaces.

LEARN IT!

Calculate **total assets** using this formula:

total assets = fixed assets + current assets

LEARN IT!

Net current assets are an indication of the business's ability to pay its current liabilities or debts. Calculate **net current assets** using this formula:

net current assets = current assets − current liabilities

LEARN IT!

Assets are what the business **owns** and liabilities are what the business **owes**. Calculate **net assets** using this formula:

net assets = total assets − total liabilities

Revision Guide
pages 31, 36

Watch out!

Use figures from the statement of financial position in question 4(a) to complete these calculations. Double-check your maths.

Hint

Show your working. You may be awarded marks for your calculation, even if your final answer is incorrect.

LEARN IT!

The liquidity ratio uses the value of current assets **without** the inventory. Stock cannot be used to pay debts (unless sold and converted into cash). A business needs to know if it has sufficient cash to pay its debts.

Hint

If a business has insufficient cash to pay its current liabilities, including money owed to suppliers, it must **increase its cash reserves**. Think about whether cash reserves can be increased using resources in the business. Also, consider ways to get cash into the business more quickly.

(b) Calculate (i) the current ratio and (ii) the liquid capital ratio for the business's first six months of operation, using the following formulas.

$$\text{current ratio} = \frac{\text{current assets}}{\text{current liabilities}}$$

$$\text{liquid capital ratio} = \frac{\text{current assets} - \text{inventory}}{\text{current liabilities}}$$

Show your working.

(i) Current ratio = ...

1 mark

Show your working.

(ii) Liquid capital ratio = ...

1 mark

Sunita is concerned about the impact on the business of the liquid capital ratio you have calculated.

(c) Give **two** actions she could take to improve the business's liquid capital ratio.

1 ....

....

2 ....

....

2 marks

Total for Activity 4 = 8 marks

Activity 5

Sunita has started to plan the expansion of her business. She has asked you to help by looking at the financial implications of expanding the business. First you need to consider the costs and revenue of introducing the new product range.

5 (a) Sunita has asked you to identify the fixed costs and variable costs.

(i) Give **one** example of a fixed cost.

....

....

1 mark

(ii) Give **one** example of a variable cost.

....

....

1 mark

Sunita has started to look at fixed and variable costs at different levels of output. She has calculated variable costs at £1.75 per unit.

(b) Fill in the shaded boxes to complete the following table.

Number of pieces of jewellery produced	100	200
Fixed costs	£1500	(ii) ....
Variable costs	(i)	£350
Total costs	£1675	(iii) ....

3 marks

Practice assessment

2

Revision Guide
pages 21–22

Hint

'Give' means you need to briefly recall some information. Try to use business key terms where appropriate.

Hint

A fixed cost does not change with output, whereas variable costs do vary with output.

LEARN IT!

To calculate **total costs:**

total costs = total fixed costs + total variable costs

LEARN IT!

To calculate **total variable costs:**

total variable costs = variable cost per unit × number of units produced

Hint

A variable cost of £1.75 per unit means it costs £1.75 for each piece of jewellery produced. Fixed costs remain the same irrespective of output.

Watch out!

Make sure you know the formulas for calculating total costs and total variable costs because they will not be provided in the assessment.

Revision Guide
page 45

Hint

At the break-even point, **total costs equal total revenue**.

Hint

Read the question carefully. Look for the key figures needed to complete the break-even chart: fixed costs, variable cost per unit, selling price and planned sales (amount to be produced).

Hint

The total revenue at the break-even level of sales is where the total cost line **intersects** the total revenue line. The margin of safety is the area above this.

LEARN IT!

The **margin of safety** is the total number of sales that can be lost before the business starts to make a loss. It is calculated by the formula:

margin of safety = sales at the break-even point – actual or planned sales

Watch out!

You will not be given the formula for the margin of safety in the assessment, so you must learn it.

Hint

If fixed costs increase, the fixed cost line moves upwards.

The break-even chart for the new jewellery range is shown below.

(c) Label the chart with the total revenue generated at the break-even point, if the selling price of the jewellery is £13.75/unit.

1 mark

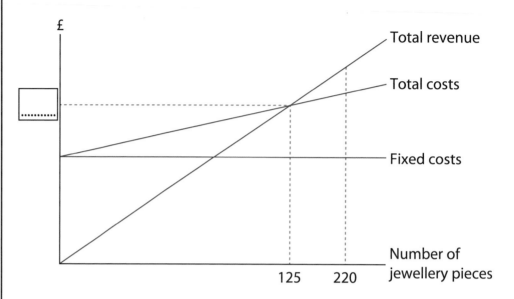

(d) From the information contained in the break-even chart, state the following:

(i) the number of pieces of jewellery that must be sold for the business to break even

.... units

1 mark

(ii) the margin of safety **in units** if the business plans to sell 220 units

.... units

1 mark

(e) Explain the effect on the break-even point if fixed costs increase.

....

....

1 mark

Total for Activity 5 = 9 marks

Activity 6

The final section of Sunita's business plan will include the cash flow forecast relating to the new jewellery range.

6 (a) Complete the following cash flow forecast for Sunita's business.

	January £	February £	March £
Cash inflows			
Bracelet sales	1000	1100	1150
Necklace sales	2500	2750	3325
Total inflows	3500	3850	4475
Cash outflows			
Salary	1000	1000	1000
Interest on business loan	125	125	125
Other costs	2250	3750	2125
Total outflow	3375	4875	3250
Net cash flow	125	(ii) ……….	1225
Opening balance	200	325	(iii) …………
Closing balance	(i) ………..	−700	525

3 marks

Revision Guide
pages 39, 51

LEARN IT!

To calculate the **closing balance**, add the net cash flow to the opening balance. Remember to subtract any negative figures.

Watch out!

A cash flow forecast looks into the **future** and is based upon a business's assumptions about future revenue and costs. A cash flow statement shows cash flow in the past.

Revision Guide
pages 49, 51

(b) Explain **one** difficulty faced by Sunita when forecasting the cash inflows of her business.

....

....

....

....

....

....

3 marks

(c) Explain **one** advantage and **one** disadvantage of using retained profit as a source of finance.

Advantage ....

....

....

....

Disadvantage ....

....

....

....

4 marks

Total for Activity 6 = 10 marks

Activity 7

Having thought about the financial aspects of her business plan, Sunita is now considering how she could successfully launch her new jewellery range. She has asked your advice on promoting the new product range.

7 (a) Explain **two** ways in which the target market influences the promotional campaign.

1 ....

....

....

....

2 ....

....

....

....

4 marks

Revision Guide
pages 10, 11–13

Hint

You need to identify the characteristics of Sunita's target market. Why is it important to identify these characteristics when deciding on promotional methods?

(b) Explain how an understanding of market segmentation could help Sunita plan her promotional activities.

....

....

....

....

2 marks

Hint

Market segments are **demographic, geographic, psychographic** and **behavioural**. Say why it's important to understand these segments before planning promotional activities.

Revision Guide
pages 4–7

Hint

'Evaluate' means you need to consider the strengths and weaknesses of sales promotions and personal selling for Sunita's business. Justify your conclusion about the best method for Sunita's business by stating reasons.

Hint

Think about the product and the business's relationship with its existing customers.

Hint

Reread the information you have been given about Sunita throughout this assessment paper. Use the information to show the depth of your understanding.

Sunita is currently considering the promotional methods she will use to promote her new jewellery range. She has a limited budget and has decided to focus her promotion on either **sales promotions** or **personal selling**.

(c) Evaluate these **two** methods of promotion.

In your answer you should include:

- an analysis of the key advantages and disadvantages of each method for promoting her enterprise
- a conclusion which recommends the best method to use for Sunita's new jewellery range.

....

....

....

....

....

....

....

....

....

....

....

....

....

....

....

....

....

....

....

....

....

....

....

....

....

....

....

....

....

....

....

....

....

....

....

....

....

....

....

....

Hint

You must only refer to the two methods given in the question: **sales promotion** and **personal selling**.

Hint

Remember to finish your answer with a conclusion that recommends the best method for Sunita's jewellery enterprise. Justify your recommendation by explaining the benefit it will give to the business.

6 marks

Total for Activity 7 = 12 marks

TOTAL FOR PAPER = 60 MARKS

Revision Guide
pages 52–65

Prepare

Read the scenario carefully and **underline** any key information. Make sure you revisit this scenario throughout the assessment to ensure your answers are relevant to Ashley's service business.

Prepare

In your actual assessment, you might find it useful to make a few notes in the margin, so that you can link different aspects of the scenario to specific questions in the assessment.

Hint

This scenario describes a business that is selling a **service**. Businesses that specialise in providing services have to put customer service at the centre of all their promotional activities.

Hint

When dealing with a service business, think of those promotional activities that can enhance the brand, develop a unique selling point and meet customer expectations.

Practice assessment 3

Answer ALL questions.
Write your answers in the spaces provided.

Some activities in this paper must be answered with a cross in a box ☒. If you change your mind about an answer, put a line through the box ☒ and then put a cross in another box ☒.

The activities in this paper are based on this scenario.
You should read this scenario carefully before you start the activities.
Complete all the activities.

Scenario

Ashley organised a number of social events at his college, including dances and talent contests. As a result, he has excellent contacts in the entertainment business. Recently, Ashley was approached by the head teacher of a local secondary school to organise the school's end-of-year Prom Night. The event was very successful. Now a number of other local schools want Ashley to organise their Prom Nights. Ashley is keen to use his experience to start a party planner business which will be called *Let Me Entertain You*.

Ashley plans to offer a wide range of services, including printing invitations, hiring accommodation, organising entertainment and supplying personalised novelty products, such as fancy dress outfits. Ashley has secured a business loan and has asked for your help on the financial aspects of the business, as well as advising on promotional activities.

Activity 1

Ashley's plans involve setting up a financial record-keeping system which can be used to track customer orders, monitor payments to suppliers and provide information to the business's accountants when the end-of-year financial statements are prepared.

1   (a)   A document contains a financial summary of the goods ordered, purchased or returned by the customer over a period of time, usually one month.

Identify the name of this document.

☐ A   Credit note

☐ B   Invoice

☐ C   Purchase order

☐ D   Statement of account

`1 mark`

(b)   The flow chart shows the process of a purchase order sent by Ashley's business to one of its suppliers. Insert the following financial documents into the flow chart.

- Receipt
- Delivery note
- Credit note

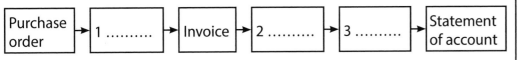

| Purchase order | → | 1 ……… | → | Invoice | → | 2 ……… | → | 3 ……… | → | Statement of account |

`3 marks`

Revision Guide
page 14

Prepare

Make sure you have revised all the **key terminology**. You need to know the purpose of all of the main sales and purchasing documents.

Hint

'Identify' means you need to select information from the choices given.

Hint

Mark your answer clearly in the box provided so that the examiner can identify your chosen response.

Prepare

Learn the order of the documents that are used in a credit sale. Ensure that you understand the purpose of each document.

Hint

In question 1(b), 'insert' means to write the correct word from the list in the appropriate box in the flow chart.

Watch out!

Double-check your answer to make sure you have filled in the boxes correctly.

Revision Guide
pages 4, 17, 19

Watch out!

Read and understand the scenario to **identify the correct figures** for the calculation. You are given details of the discounts for orders of different values. Make sure you apply the correct discount. Subtract the discount from the subtotal.

Hint

'**Calculate**' means you will need to complete a calculation as part of the answer.

Hint

'**Give**' questions are like 'state' or 'identify' questions. You need to provide a correct statement, not an explanation.

Hint

Online payments are made with a credit or debit card.

Explore

The **promotional mix** uses different promotional methods. Some methods encourage consumers to buy products. Others create a positive brand image.

Mr Peter Craddock has sent in a purchase order to Let Me Entertain You. Ashley has started to write out the invoice. He has asked you to complete the invoice based on the following information:

- 5% discount on orders up to £1500
- 10% discount on orders over £1500
- VAT is payable at a rate of 20%

(c) Calculate the missing information and insert your answers into the shaded boxes in the invoice.

3 marks

INVOICE

Peter Craddock
Hillchester
Tollinbridge
TO5 4PY

Date: 12 April
Invoice number: 347/89/YE

Please send payment to:
Let Me Entertain You
47 Cobham Drive
Everley
EV8 8TY

Description	Quantity	Unit price	Total price
Party invites	125	£1.75	£218.75
Balloons	250	£0.75	£187.50
Buffet food	100	£5.25	£525.00
Musical entertainment	1	£400	£400.00
		Subtotal	£1331.25
		Discount	(i) ....
		Subtotal after discount	£1264.69
		VAT @ 20%	(ii) ....
		Total payable	(iii) ....

Let Me Entertain You will have a strong online presence, which will include a website. Online payments will be possible.

(d) Give **one** reason why Ashley may also accept cash payments from his customers.

....

1 mark

(e) Identify the main purpose of any sales promotion.

....

1 mark

Total for Activity 1 = 9 marks

Activity 2

Ashley has asked you to check a purchase order for balloons and streamers.

Goods required	List price	Number required
Balloons	£0.50 each	100
Streamers	£1.25 each	225

2 (a) Calculate the **three** errors in the following order.

Item description	Order code	Price per unit	Number required	Total price £	Total price p
Streamers	245/S	£1.25	225	271	50
Balloons	412/B	£0.50	100	50	00
			Subtotal	328	45
			VAT @ 20%	67	75
			Total	**397**	**50**

Error item	Original amount	Corrected amount
		(i) ....
		(ii) ....
		(iii) ....

3 marks

Hint

Check the information and the calculations in the purchase order to find the errors. Then complete the table.

Explore

It is good practice to double-check all financial documents before they are sent out to customers and suppliers. If the documents contain inaccuracies, this could impact on a business's cash flow and create disputes.

Watch out!

Some of the figures in this purchase order are actually correct. You will still have to work out all the values to identify the incorrect values.

Prepare

You are allowed to use a calculator. Remember to bring one for the assessment.

Revision Guide
pages 15, 16, 31

LEARN IT!

Bookkeeping is the process of maintaining accurate records of a business's cash inflows and cash outflows. Most businesses maintain computerised records of their costs and revenue which helps to ensure the data is up to date and accurate.

Hint

Look for the words in bold. In question 1(b), you are only asked for **one** reason.

Hint

Question 1(c) expects two distinct answers, as indicated by the numbering.

Hint

Question 1(d) is an 'explain' question and requires you to identify two reasons. You should justify why each reason is relevant to the bank.

Hint

The **statement of financial position** shows the value of the business, and all its assets and liabilities. Think about why this information might be of interest to Ashley's bank.

(b) Give **one** reason why Ashley should keep financial records of his business.

....

....

1 mark

(c) Identify **two** types of current assets that appear in a statement of financial position.

1 ....

2 ....

2 marks

(d) Explain **two** reasons why Ashley's bank may be interested in his business's statement of financial position.

1 ....

....

....

....

2 ....

....

....

....

4 marks

Total for Activity 2 = 10 marks

Activity 3

Ashley organised an event at a local community centre. He has asked you to work out how much profit the event made.

3 (a) Complete the following statement of comprehensive income by filling in the shaded boxes.

Statement of comprehensive income COMMUNITY CENTRE EVENT		
	£	£
Sales revenue (cash sales)		1750
Cost of sales		(i) ....
Gross profit		**1150**
Expenses		
Musical equipment hire	300	
DJ	200	
Streamers	135	
Balloons	50	
Buffet food	175	
Total expenses	**860**	
Net profit or loss		(ii) ....

2 marks

(b) Explain **one** way Ashley could have increased the net profit generated by the event.

....

....

....

....

2 marks

Revision Guide
pages 25, 29

Hint

'**Complete**' means to carry out the calculation and insert numbers in the boxes.

LEARN IT!

Use this formula to calculate **gross profit**:

gross profit = sales revenue – cost of sales

LEARN IT!

Use this formula to calculate **net profit**:

net profit = gross profit – business expenses

Hint

Read the question carefully. You are asked to give **one** way of increasing the net profit – don't list more than one. Give one way and develop your explanation.

Hint

Profit is influenced by **business costs** and **sales revenue**. Controlling costs is important. If costs increase, profit reduces. Businesses can even make losses.

Hint

Revenue can be increased by putting up the price of the service so consumers pay more. However, they may decide to purchase cheaper services from other businesses.

Revision Guide
pages 31, 32

Hint

A business sets financial performance targets so it can monitor its performance. Targets can help a business identify and address problems.

Prepare

Practise completing the statement of comprehensive income and the statement of financial position. You should know the information in each and how to carry out the calculations correctly.

Watch out!

This is an **extract** from a statement of financial position. The **complete** statement of financial position would include information on money invested by the owner (owner's funds), plus any profit made by the business in the financial year.

LEARN IT!

To calculate **net current assets**, you need to extract the figures for current assets and current liabilities:

net current assets = current assets − current liabilities

Ashley wants to set financial performance targets. He will base the targets on projected figures for the business's first year of operations.

He must ensure that the business has sufficient funds to pay suppliers.

(c) Complete the following extract from Ashley's projected statement of financial position. Insert the correct figures into the shaded boxes.

Extract from projected statement of financial position – *Let Me Entertain You*		
	£	£
Assets		
Fixed assets	(i)	
Current assets		
Inventory	6000	
Cash in bank	1500	
Total assets		11 000
Liabilities		
Current liabilities	2000	
Long-term liabilities	(ii)	
Total liabilities		3000
Net current assets		(iii) ....

3 marks

(d) Calculate (i) the current ratio and (ii) the liquid capital ratio for the business from the projected statement of financial position, using the following formulas.

$$\text{current ratio} = \frac{\text{current assets}}{\text{current liabilities}}$$

$$\text{liquid capital ratio} = \frac{\text{current assets} - \text{inventory}}{\text{current liabilities}}$$

Show your working.

(i) Current ratio = ...

1 mark

Show your working.

(ii) Liquid capital ratio = ...

1 mark

(e) Give **one** reason why Ashley should be concerned about the business's liquid capital ratio.

....

....

1 mark

Total for Activity 3 = 10 marks

Revision Guide
page 36

LEARN IT!

Financial targets can be set using information from the statement of comprehensive income (profit margins) and the statement of financial position (liquidity ratios).

Hint

Calculate current ratio and liquidity ratio using the formula and data given. Include your working.

LEARN IT!

Profit margins are expressed as a percentage. Liquidity is expressed as a ratio. A ratio shows how much of one thing there is compared to another.

Hint

Current assets represent the business's ability to pay its debts in the short term. Current liabilities show how much short-term debt the business has.

Explore

Loans increase a business's liabilities. If the business uses short-term loans to address cash flow problems, its current liabilities increase and its net current assets (current assets − current liabilities) reduce.

Enterprise
REVISION GUIDE
Revision Guide
page 45

LEARN IT!

Use this formula to calculate **profit or loss**:

profit (or loss) = total revenue − total costs

At break-even, total revenue equals total costs.

Watch out!

Use a minus sign for a negative figure.

LEARN IT!

Use this formula to calculate **total costs**:

total costs = fixed costs + variable costs

LEARN IT!

Break-even assumes all costs remain the same (whereas the business might obtain discounts for bulk purchases) and revenue is a straight line (although the business may offer discounts to some customers).

Hint

When total costs are greater than total revenue, the business makes a **loss**; if total revenue is greater than total costs, it makes a **profit**. Think about whether the shaded area on the break-even chart shows a profit or a loss.

Activity 4

Ashley asks you to draw a break-even chart so he can work out the profit or loss at different levels of ticket sales for a new event he is planning at the local Town Hall.

4 (a) Complete the following table by filling in the shaded boxes.

Ticket sales	Fixed costs	Variable costs	Total costs	Sales revenue	Profit or loss
200	£3200	£100	(i)	£1700	−£1600
300	£3200	£150	£3350	£2550	(ii) ....
400	(iii)	£200	£3400	£3400	£0
500	£3200	£250	£3450	£4240	(iv) ....

4 marks

Break-even chart for _Let Me Entertain You_

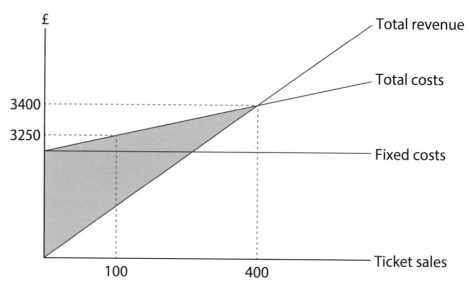

(b) State the total costs of selling 100 tickets.

....

1 mark

(c) Explain what is represented by the shaded area.

....

....

....

....

2 marks

(d) Explain what would happen to the break-even point in the following circumstances:

(i) Ashley decided to reduce the price of the tickets.

....

....

....

....

2 marks

(ii) The cost of hiring the Town Hall was reduced.

....

....

....

....

2 marks

Total for Activity 4 = 11 marks

Revision Guide
page 46

Revision Guide
pages 39–42

LEARN IT!

Use this formula to calculate **net cash flow**:

net cash flow = cash inflows – cash outflows

Hint

Double-check your calculations before entering figures into the cash flow forecast. Make sure you enter the numbers in the correct spaces.

Hint

For question 5(b), think about the implications for the business if cash outflows are greater than cash inflows.

Hint

Cash is an important element of a business's liquidity.

Hint

Inventory is stock. In Ashley's business, stock is the goods purchased from suppliers and used in the events.

Explore

A business should update its cash flow forecast if it takes out a loan, because it will have an additional cash outflow to meet its monthly repayments. Some external events cause increased cash inflows (large orders) or increased cash outflows (rising costs).

Activity 5

Ashley is thinking about the cash flow of his business for the next three months. He has started a cash flow forecast and asks you to complete it for him.

5 (a) Complete the cash flow forecast by inserting the correct figures into the shaded boxes.

	October £	November £	December £
Cash inflows			
Birthday parties	4000	4300	6500
Musical shows	2500	3500	4250
Total inflows	**6500**	**7800**	**10 750**
Cash outflows			
Salary	2000	2000	2000
Purchase of supplies	3000	(ii)	5250
Other costs	1250	1875	2545
Total outflow	6250	7125	9795
Net cash flow	250	675	(iii) ....
Opening balance	(i)	700	1375
Closing balance	**700**	**1375**	**2330**

3 marks

(b) Give **one** reason why Ashley has produced a cash flow forecast.

....

1 mark

(c) Explain why Ashley might be pleased with the outcome of his cash flow forecast.

....

....

2 marks

Ashley has decided to sell off some of his inventory to generate additional cash.

(d) Explain **one** impact of selling off some of the business's inventory.

....

....

2 marks

Total for Activity 5 = 8 marks

Activity 6

In November and December, many local businesses arrange end-of-year parties for their staff. Ashley thinks there will be significant opportunities for his business. He is keen to develop a promotional campaign to maximise sales opportunities. Advertising will play a key role in the promotional campaign.

6 (a) Explain the benefits of **two** methods of advertising.

Method 1 ....

....

....

....

Method 2 ....

....

....

....

[4 marks]

(b) Explain why Ashley should create a brand image for his business.

....

....

....

....

[2 marks]

Revision Guide
pages 2–3

Hint

Identify **two different** methods of advertising and explain the benefits to the business of each one.

LEARN IT!

The purpose of advertising is to inform and persuade. The effectiveness of advertising depends on a business's understanding of its target market and the main consumer groups within the target market.

Hint

A number of factors influence the purchasing decisions of consumers. Different people have different aspirations, incomes and lifestyles.

Revision Guide
pages 6, 11

Hint

'**Assess**' means you must weigh up the advantages and disadvantages of specific business activities, such as market segmentation, and show a balanced argument.

Prepare

It's a good idea to plan your answer to a long question before you start to write.

(c) Assess the importance of market segmentation for the success of Ashley's promotional campaign.

....

....

....

....

....

....

....

....

....

....

....

....

....

....

....

....

....

....

....

(c) ....

....

....

....

....

....

....

....

....

....

....

....

....

....

....

....

....

....

....

....

....

....

....

....

....

....

....

Hint

Refer to all the information you learned about the business in earlier parts of the scenario and extra information given with activities, so that you can be sure that your answer is focused on Ashley's party planner business.

Hint

Think about how understanding his target market could impact Ashley's choice of promotional campaign. Link this to the success of his business – for example, reaching his market, pricing and so on.

6 marks

Total for Activity 6 = 12 marks

TOTAL FOR PAPER = 60 MARKS

Revision Guide
page 53

Time it!

This Practice Assessment allows you to practise writing answers in a set time of two hours. Check with your tutor about the timing of your actual assessment.

Hint

Read the scenario carefully and highlight key points. Your answers must be in the context of the correct business – *Sparks & Cables* or *Eazicut Sales*. Double-check which business each question asks about.

Hint

Think about the features of the *Eazicut* that give the product an advantage over similar products produced by Jarek's competitors.

Hint

Although Jarek has started a new business, there may be advantages in using *Sparks & Cables* to identify the potential target market for any promotional activities, including sales promotions.

Practice assessment 4

> Answer ALL questions.
> Write your answers in the spaces provided.

Some activities in this paper must be answered with a cross in a box ☒. If you change your mind about an answer, put a line through the box ☒ and then put a cross in another box ☒.

The activities in this paper are based on this scenario.
You should read this scenario carefully before you start the activities.
Complete all the activities.

Scenario

Jarek works in his father's business, *Sparks & Cables*. The company manufactures tools for the construction industry. Jarek is part of the product design team. He has been working on the design of a new low-cost tool, the *Eazicut*, which will enable electricians to install electrical cables in half the time they currently take to complete the work.

Jarek is responsible for drawing up the financial plans for manufacturing the product. This includes obtaining components and determining a price for the *Eazicut* that will enable the business to make a profit. He will also be responsible for promoting the product to electricians in the construction industry. The *Eazicut* will be manufactured and supplied by a new offshoot business, *Eazicut Sales*, which Jarek will manage.

Jarek has asked for your help with the financial and promotional aspects to ensure the success of the new product.

RUINS NIVEL YOUR AWARD
Enterprise
REVISION
GUIDE
Revision Guide
pages 14, 29

Activity 1

Jarek wants to keep financial records relating to the sales and costs of *Eazicut Sales*, so that he can work out if the new product is profitable.

1 (a) Identify which of the following financial documents would show the profit made by Jarek's business.

☐ A   Cash flow forecast

☐ B   Cash flow statement

☐ C   Statement of comprehensive income

☐ D   Statement of account

1 mark

Jarek has produced the following flow chart of the documents used in the business. He has asked you to check it for him.

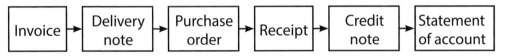

| Invoice | → | Delivery note | → | Purchase order | → | Receipt | → | Credit note | → | Statement of account |

(b) State which **two** documents are in the wrong order in the flow chart.

1 ....

2 ....

2 marks

Time it!

Don't spend too much time on one-mark questions. If you don't know the answer, move on and come back to the question when you have finished the assessment.

Hint

In a **multiple-choice question**, discount any options that are incorrect before carefully selecting the right answer.

Hint

For short-answer questions like 'state', 'identify' or 'give', provide precise answers using correct terminology from the specification.

Hint

Some of the documents are already in the right order. Tick the documents that are correct to quickly identify those that are not.

Revision Guide
pages 2, 17, 18

Hint

The question asks for **financial information** so don't identify features such as customer name or date.

Hint

The *Eazicut* is aimed at professional electricians with their own businesses. For this '**explain**' question, consider how using more efficient equipment could help a business.

(c) Identify **two** pieces of financial information that would appear on an invoice.

1 ....

....

2 ....

....

2 marks

(d) Give **one** reason why Jarek would issue receipts to his customers.

....

....

1 mark

(e) Explain, using the information in the scenario, **one** financial benefit of the *Eazicut* that Jarek could highlight in his promotional material aimed at electricians.

....

....

....

....

2 marks

Total Activity 1 = 8 marks

Activity 2

A recent order sent to *Drapers Electrical Stores* contained three damaged *Eazicut* tools. These were returned to *Eazicut Sales*.

2 (a) Complete a credit note to be sent to *Drapers Electrical Stores*. The price of the *Eazicut* tool is £25.95 plus VAT at 20%.

Eazicut Sales
CREDIT NOTE

Drapers Electrical Stores
Brillington
BR9 6RT

Date: 12 April
Credit note number: Cr/342/DES

Description	Quantity	Unit price	Total price
Eazicut tool	3	£25.95	(i) ....
		VAT	(ii) ....
		Total credit	(iii) ....

3 marks

(b) Explain how *Drapers Electrical Stores* will be able to access the amount of credit they are owed by Jarek's business.

....

....

....

....

2 marks

(c) Give **one** impact on Jarek's statement of comprehensive income if the money received from the sales of the *Eazicut* is not accurately recorded.

....

....

1 mark

REVISE BTEC TECH AWARD
Enterprise
REVISION
GUIDE

Revision Guide
pages 18, 29

Hint

'**Complete**' means you need to carry out calculations and insert correct figures in the right boxes of the credit note.

Hint

Make sure you account for the correct number of damaged *Eazicut* tools.

LEARN IT!

A **credit note** is completed by the supplier and sent to the customer. It lists goods that have been returned by the customer to the supplier.

Hint

Money on the credit note is refunded to the customer. Customers make a monthly payment for all orders **minus** any credit notes.

Hint

For question 2(c), consider the information in the statement of comprehensive income and its importance to the business.

Time it!

Don't spend too long on short-answer questions. Save time to develop the longer answers at the end of the assessment.

Revision Guide
pages 10, 19, 20

REVISE BTEC TECH AWARD
Enterprise
REVISION
GUIDE

LEARN IT!

Factors that influence
choice of payment method
include convenience,
security, cost, technology,
lifestyle and ability to pay.

Hint

Credit card companies
pay for goods on behalf of
consumers, who then have
a period of time to pay
back their debt. Consider
how credit card companies
make a profit.

Hint

Identify an advantage
for the business. Then
develop the point using
a **connecting phrase** like
'such as' or 'therefore'.

 **Explore**

Market size can be
measured in two ways:

1. market value (potential
   value of sales)

2. market volume
   (potential number of
   consumers or potential
   number of sales).

Time it!

Allocate your time evenly
across the assessment.
As a guide, allow two
minutes per mark,
including thinking time.

Jarek operates his business in a business-to-business (B2B) market.
He sells the Eazicut tool to electrical wholesalers and self-employed
electricians. Many of his customers pay by credit card.

(d) (i) Explain **one** advantage to Jarek's customers of paying by credit
card.

....

....

....

....

2 marks

(ii) Explain **one** disadvantage to Jarek of offering credit card
payments to his customers.

....

....

....

....

2 marks

(e) Explain **one** advantage to Jarek's business of marketing the *Eazicut*
tool to the business-to-consumer (B2C) market.

....

....

....

....

2 marks

Total for Activity 2 = 12 marks

Activity 3

After a year of trading, Jarek wants to compare the performance of his business, *Eazicut Sales*, with that of his father's business, *Sparks & Cables*. Jarek has drawn up a statement of comprehensive income for the first year of trading.

3 (a) Calculate the missing figures in the statement of comprehensive income for *Eazicut Sales*. Insert the figures into the correct shaded boxes.

Statement of comprehensive income Year 1 *Eazicut Sales*		
	£	£
Sales		55 250
Cost of sales		31 500
Gross profit		(i)..............
Expenses		
Rent	6750	
Promotional leaflets	1225	
Telephone	1450	
Office expenses	2700	
Transport	1250	
Total expenses	13 375	
Net profit		(ii)............

2 marks

(b) Calculate (i) gross profit margin and (ii) net profit margin of *Eazicut Sales* using these formulas:

$$\text{gross profit margin} = \frac{\text{gross profit}}{\text{sales revenue}} \times 100$$

$$\text{net profit margin} = \frac{\text{net profit}}{\text{sales revenue}} \times 100$$

Show your working.

(i) Gross profit margin = ... %

1 mark

Show your working.

(ii) Net profit margin = ... %

1 mark

Revision Guide
pages 29, 34–35

Hint

Always **double-check your calculations**. You will also need the correct gross and net profit figures to calculate the answer to question 3(b).

Prepare

Practise calculating the different formulas to make sure you know how to use them properly.

Hint

Extract figures from the statement of comprehensive income for the calculations in question 3(b).

Prepare

Sales revenue is in the formulas for both gross and net profit margins. Practise inserting different values for sales revenue to calculate profit margins. You will see what happens to profit margins when sales revenue increases or decreases.

Time it!

You will be faster using a calculator to do calculations.

Watch out!

If you are required to multiply by 100 as part of the formula then the answer should be expressed as a %.

Revision Guide
pages 30, 34–35

Hint

Net profit has a monetary value whereas net profit margin is a percentage. These terms tell you different things about a business's performance.

Hint

One business may have a larger net profit but a lower net profit margin than another. How do business expenses affect these two measures?

Hint

'State' questions demand clear and concise answers.

Hint

Consider the effect of cash sales and credit sales on cash flow.

Businesses can improve their performance by comparing themselves to successful competitors and introducing similar practices. Successful business practices reduce costs without lowering quality and increase sales revenue.

Time it!

Check the time throughout the assessment to ensure you are on target to finish the paper.

Jarek is unsure about the difference between the net profit and the net profit *margin* of his business.

(c) Explain the difference between net profit and net profit margin for Jarek's business.

....

....

....

....

2 marks

The net profit margin of *Sparks & Cables* is 22.5%.

(d) Give **one** reason for the difference in the net profit margins between Jarek's business and *Sparks & Cables*.

....

....

1 mark

(e) State **one** difference between a cash sale and a credit sale.

....

....

1 mark

Total for Activity 3 = 8 marks

Activity 4

Jarek has plans to produce a cheaper version of the *Eazicut* tool, the *Eazicut Junior*. This will be targeted at homeowners and DIY enthusiasts. Jarek will need to rent a new warehouse to store the metal sheets used in the manufacture of the *Eazicut*.

He wants to work out how many tools he will need to sell in order to make a profit.

4 (a) Give **one** example of a fixed cost and **one** example of a variable cost which will arise from production of the new tool.

Fixed cost ....

1 mark

Variable cost ....

1 mark

Jarek asks you to work out the costs and revenue of the *Eazicut Junior*. You will use these to work out the break-even point at different price levels. He gives you the following financial information.

Fixed costs	£2250
Variable costs per unit	£3.50
Price of the *Eazicut Junior*	£8

(b) Calculate the number of *Eazicut Junior* tools that would need to be sold in order to break even. Use this formula:

$$\frac{\text{fixed costs}}{\text{selling price per unit} - \text{variable cost per unit}}$$

Show your working.

Break-even point = ... units

1 mark

Watch out!

Read the additional information. Jarek is moving into the B2C (business-to-consumer) market. He currently operates B2B (business-to-business) as he markets to professional electricians in the construction industry.

Hint

For question 4(a), you only need to give examples of **one** fixed and **one** variable cost. An explanation is not required.

Hint

Use the values in the table and the formula to calculate the break-even point in question 4(b).

Explore

Calculate different break-even points by adjusting the selling price. Analyse the difference in break-even points when the selling price changes.

Time it!

It is a great idea to practise answering assessment questions against the clock, so you are well prepared to work under exam conditions.

Revision Guide
page 43

LEARN IT!

To calculate the **sales revenue** at the break-even point, multiply the number of units by the price per unit.

Hint

Fixed and variable costs are the same but the price is reduced to £6. You need to calculate the new break-even point for a selling price of £6. Then find the difference in the number of units at the break-even points for selling prices of £8 and £6.

Hint

Show your working in the boxes provided. You may gain marks for a correct calculation, even if your final answer is wrong.

Time it!

Don't spend too long on short-answer questions. You will need a few minutes left at the end to check over your answers.

(c) Calculate the total revenue at the break-even point.

Show your working.

Total revenue at the break-even point = £ ....

1 mark

Jarek wants to consider the impact on the business if the price of the *Eazicut Junior* was reduced to £6.

(d) Calculate the *additional* number of *Eazicut Junior* tools that would need to be sold in order to break even. Refer to question 4(b) for the formula and use the same values for fixed and variable costs.

Show your working.

Additional sales to break even .... units

2 marks

Jarek decides to market the *Eazicut Junior* at £8 and prepares a break-even chart. He plans to sell 700 units. Fixed and variable costs are shown in the table in question 4(a).

Jarek's break-even chart for the new *Eazicut Junior* is shown below.

(e) Complete the break-even chart by inserting the correct details into the shaded boxes.

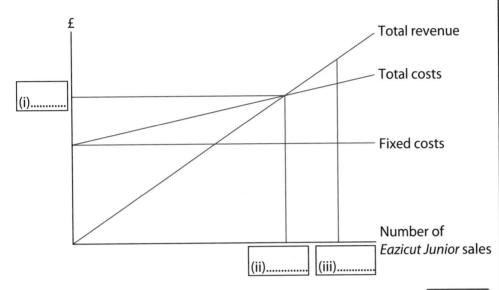

3 marks

(f) Explain **one** limitation of break-even analysis.

....

....

....

....

....

....

3 marks

Total for Activity 4 = 12 marks

Revision Guide
pages 44, 47

Watch out!

Read the additional information carefully. Sales of 700 units is above the break-even point.

Hint

'**Complete**' means you have to insert data you have been given and data from your previous answers into the correct boxes.

LEARN IT!

The total revenue line starts at the origin of the graph (0, 0). There is no revenue when there are no sales. The fixed cost line is located above the origin on the vertical axis.

Hint

A business may obtain discounts if it buys materials in bulk. The variable cost per unit changes at different production levels.

 **Time it!**

You have six minutes for this three-mark '**explain**' question. Make a point, justify the point and expand on your justification.

REVISION GUIDE

Revision Guide
page 39

Activity 5

Jarek must ensure he has sufficient cash coming into the business. He has prepared a cash flow forecast for the first month of trading and asks you to check it for accuracy.

Item	January £
Eazicut sales	3250
Eazicut Junior sales	400
Total inflows	**3750**
Salary	1500
Purchase of metal sheeting	2500
Other costs	1150
Total outflow	5150
Net cash flow	−1200
Opening balance	2000
Closing balance	700

5 (a) Identify the **three** errors that appear in the cash flow forecast for January and calculate the correct figures.

Item in the cash flow forecast	Correct amount (£)
(i)	£............................
(ii)	£............................
(iii)	£............................

3 marks

(b) Explain the difference between a cash flow forecast and a cash flow statement.

....

....

....

....

2 marks

Jarek considers that he may need to generate additional cash in order to support his business.

(c) Give **one** way Jarek could generate income from the assets in his business.

....

....

1 mark

Revision Guide
pages 19, 21

Hint

You only need to provide a short statement for this one-mark question. You do not need to explain your answer.

Jarek is planning to develop a website. He wants his customers to be able to purchase the *Eazicut Junior* online.

(d) Explain **two** advantages to Jarek's customers of being able to make online purchases.

1 ....

....

....

....

2 ....

....

....

....

4 marks

Total for Activity 5 = 10 marks

Hint

Give **two different** advantages and back up each one with an expansion point that identifies the impact of the advantage for the consumer. You could write: 'This is an advantage because ...'

LEARN IT!

Jarek must keep his website up to date so that customers have access to the correct information when they are ordering goods.

 **Time it!**

Look at the writing space and mark allocation to help you work out how long to spend on the answer. Question 5(d) is worth four marks so allow yourself eight minutes including planning time.

Revision Guide
pages 6, 9

Hint

The purpose of promotional activity is to increase sales or promote the brand.

Activity 6

Jarek wants to keep his promotional costs low when he launches the *Eazicut Junior* to the market. He has asked your advice on how to make the promotions as cost-effective as possible.

6 (a) Explain **two** factors that Jarek should take into account when deciding which promotion methods to use.

1 ....

....

....

....

2 ....

....

....

....

4 marks

Make a **plan** for longer answers to ensure you make the best use of your time.

Hint

'Evaluate' means you need to consider the strengths and weaknesses of **direct marketing** for Jarek's business and come to a justified conclusion about the best method. Use information from throughout the assessment to show depth of understanding.

There are a number of methods a business can use to influence the purchasing decisions of consumers. One such method is direct marketing.

(b) Evaluate the benefits of direct marketing to the successful launch of the *Eazicut Junior* in the B2C (business-to-customer) market.

In your answer you should include:

• an analysis of the key features of direct marketing

• a conclusion which recommends how direct marketing could influence the promotional methods used to launch the *Eazicut Junior* into the B2C market.

....

....

....

....

....

....

....

....

....
....
....
....
....
....
....
....
....
....
....
....
....
....
....
....
....
....
....
....
....
....
....

Hint

Your conclusion should highlight the benefits, costs and potential limitations of direct marketing.

Time it!

Leave at least five minutes to check your paper. Check as many answers as possible, making changes if necessary.

Time it!

Review how long it took you to complete the assessment. Think about how you could allocate your time differently to improve your performance.

6 marks

Total for Activity 6 = 10 marks

TOTAL FOR PAPER = 60 MARKS

Answers

Use this section to check your answers.
- For questions with clear correct answers, these are provided. If there are alternative correct answers, these are given.
- For questions where answers may be individual or require longer answers, example answers are provided to indicate key points you could include in your answer, or how your answer could be structured. **Your answer should be written using sentences and paragraphs**, and might include some of these points but not necessarily all of them.

> The questions and sample answers are provided to help you revise content and skills. Ask your tutor or check the Pearson website for the most up-to-date Sample Assessment Material, past papers and mark schemes for an indication of the actual assessment and what this requires of you. Details of the actual assessment may change so always make sure you are up to date.

Practice assessment 1

(pages 1–13)

1 (a) Credit note: Issued by the supplier to the customer so that money owed to the customer can be used to purchase goods at a later date.
Purchase order: Sent to a supplier by the customer, this lists the products required from the supplier.
Delivery note: Sent by the supplier to the customer as acknowledgement that the order has been received.

(b) (i) The Game Store   (ii) £380 (Subtotal)
(iii) £456 (Total payable)

(c) Individual response. For example:
Climate Solutions may experience cash flow problems. This could mean Sam is not able to pay her business expenses.

2 (a) (i) Subtotal: £115.00
(ii) Postage and packaging: £0.00
(iii) VAT at 20%: £23.00
(iv) Total to pay: £138.00

(b) Individual responses. For example, **two** of the following: demographic, geographic, behavioural, psychographic.

3 (a) (i) $75 \times £4 = £300$
(ii) Total costs = £1500 + 300 = £1800

(b) Individual response. For example:
1 Direct marketing can build positive associations with a brand, which could lead to repeat sales.
2 Direct marketing involves communicating directly with the customer, so a business can expose its customers to all their products or target customers more effectively for specific products.

4 (a) Break-even point: $\dfrac{3250}{20 - 3.75} = \dfrac{3250}{16.25} = 200$ board games

(b) A = total revenue; B = total costs; C = fixed costs

(c) Individual response. For example:
Public relations involves promoting a product or service, brand or enterprise by placing information about it in the media, without paying for the time or media space directly. This low-cost method of promoting Sam's *Climate Solutions* board game could have a positive impact on profits.

(d) Individual response. For example:
Sam's business customers will benefit from having an extra 30 days before they need to pay for the goods they have received, meaning that they can spread their costs.

5 (a) A cash outflow is a cash sum leaving the business, which pays for its supplies or other business costs.

(b) (i) £3950 + £1650 = £5600
(ii) £5600 − £6900 = − £1300
(iii) £1475 − £500 = £975

(c) Individual response. For example:
1 If net current assets are positive (that is, current assets are greater than current liabilities) then the business will be able to pay its short-term debts. This means that Sam can continue producing the *Climate Solutions* board game and meet customer orders.
2 If net current assets are negative (that is, current assets are less than current liabilities) then Sam will not be able to afford to purchase materials. This could impact on her ability to produce the *Climate Solutions* board game, resulting in orders being lost.

6 (a) gross profit = sales revenue − cost of sales
(b) net profit = gross profit − expenses
(c) (i) Sales revenue (Credit sales) = £13 250
(ii) Gross profit = £12 150
(iii) Total expenses = £4500
(iv) Net profit = £7650

(d) (i) Gross profit margin $= \dfrac{12\,150}{30\,000} \times 100 = 40.5\%$

(ii) Net profit margin $= \dfrac{7650}{30\,000} \times 100 = 25.5\%$

(e) Individual response. For example, **one** from:
- To increase the net profit margin, the business could reduce expenses that are not directly related to the products or services, such as office consumables.
- To increase the net profit margin, the business could take measures to reduce the cost of sales by obtaining discounts on the raw materials it purchases from suppliers, which would increase its gross profit.
- Increase sales revenue by improving the effectiveness of its promotional activities.

7 (a) Individual response. For example, **one** from:
- The business can acquire the equipment without having to pay out large amounts of money, which means that its current level of cash reserves will not be significantly reduced.
- The business returns the machinery to the leasing company at the end of the leasing period, which means that it is not left with an unwanted asset at the end of the lease agreement.

(b) Individual response. For example:
1 Income could have a positive effect on sales, because people with higher incomes may have money to spend on luxury goods such as the deluxe version of *Climate Solutions*.
2 People's social class (socio-economic group) is based on their income and type of occupation. The deluxe version of *Climate Solutions* could be targeted at those in a higher social class, who are perceived to have more disposable income to spend on non-essential items such as board games.

(c) Individual response. For example:
Face-to-face selling is a good method of personal selling for Sam's business because the salesperson is able to listen to the customer and watch their body language and signals. The salesperson can then adjust their message to demonstrate how the product solves a problem and meets customer needs, also answering any questions Sam's customer may have. However, this type of personal selling is time-consuming and requires high levels of interpersonal skills to be successful. Telephone sales are usually a faster method of personal selling than face-to-face, saving Sam's business both time and money. It also still involves personal contact with the customer, allowing questions and concerns to be addressed immediately. It can provide an aftersales service via telephone, improving the customer service offered by Sam's

business. However, this method can incur the cost of using the phone to speak to customers who are not interested in purchasing, and some customers do not like being called in their home or on their mobile phone. It doesn't allow the sales team to adapt their pitch by gauging body language, and many people have had bad experiences with telephone sales in the past, meaning they may not be receptive.

Your conclusion should state which method would be better for Sam's business, with reasoning for this choice.

Practice assessment 2
(pages 14–27)

1. (a) B: Press release
   (b) (i) Delivery note → inventory
       (ii) Purchase order → costs
       (iii) Customer invoice → revenue
   (c) To ensure that the customer pays the correct amount of money for the goods they have received, otherwise the business could experience cash flow difficulties.
   (d) Any one from: moving image, print, ambient, digital, audio

2. (a) (i) £375 + £225 = £600
       (ii) £600 − £150 = £450
       (iii) £350 + £150 = £500
       (iv) £700 − £500 = £200
   (b) One from:
       • Allowing credit card sales increases the opportunity of generating sales revenue.
       • Credit allows customers to 'buy now and pay later'.
   (c) One from:
       • Cash may be stolen.
       • A high level of security is required.

3. (a) Individual response. For example:
       1 She could try to obtain her materials from a different supplier who charges less for the materials than her current supplier. This would reduce her costs, giving greater profits.
       2 She could try to negotiate a discount from her existing supplier so that she pays less money for the same amount of materials. The savings will give her a better profit.
   (b) Two from:
       • The sale of assets would increase cash reserves, increasing the income of Sunita's business and allowing her to address any cash flow difficulties in her cash flow forecast.
       • Sunita could sell out-of-date (old) assets and use the money she receives to purchase more up-to-date (newer) equipment which would improve business efficiency.
       • The increase in income from the sale of assets could be used to purchase supplies in bulk at discount prices, which would reduce business costs.

4. (a) (i) £6500 − £3000 = £3500
       (ii) £3500 − £1500 = £2000
       (iii) £6500 − £1500 = £5000
       (iv) £5000 − £4000 = £1000
   (b) (i) Current ratio $= \dfrac{3500}{1500} = 2.33:1$
       (ii) Liquid capital ratio $= \dfrac{3500 - 2500}{1500} = \dfrac{1000}{1500} = 0.66:1$
   (c) Individual response. For example:
       1 Reduce inventory levels and convert into cash.
       2 Increase cash deposits by reducing credit terms to customers.

5. (a) (i) One from: rent, insurance, regular monthly loan repayments, salaries

       (ii) One from: materials, hourly-paid workers, electricity and energy costs
   (b) (i) Variable costs = £175 (£1.75 × 100)
       (ii) Fixed costs = £1500
       (iii) Total costs = £1500 + £350 = £1850
   (c) 125 × £13.75 = £1718.75
   (d) (i) 125 units (extracted from the break-even chart)
       (ii) 220 − 125 = 95 units
   (e) The break-even point would increase because the business would have to generate more sales to break even.

6. (a) (i) Closing balance for January = £125 (net cash flow) + £200 (opening balance) = £325
       (ii) Net cash flow for February = £3850 (total inflows) − £4875 (total outflow) = −£1025
       (iii) Opening balance for March = −£700 (from the closing balance for February)
   (b) One from:
       • It is difficult to forecast cash inflows because they are largely based on forecasting the demand for jewellery products. The demand will be influenced by a number of internal and external factors. Internal factors will include the price of the new jewellery range – if this is set too high it may put consumers off buying the product, so the actual cash inflow will be below the forecast.
       • Changes in external factors that are beyond the control of the business can influence cash inflows and mean that they vary from forecasts. For example, a competitor may enter the market, taking sales away from Sunita's business, so the actual cash inflows are below the forecast cash inflows.
   (c) Individual response. For example:
       Advantage: If Sunita retains profits, the money can be used to invest in the business so she will not have to take out a loan and pay interest.
       Disadvantage: Sunita will have less money in the business to pay for unexpected costs or emergency expenses.

7. (a) Individual response. For example:
       1 The enterprise must ensure that it has a clear understanding of its target market because promotion does not work if it does not reach and connect with the target market.
       2 To have a positive impact on sales, promotional methods must be based upon the habits of the target group, including their lifestyle and their use of social media.
   (b) Understanding how the market is segmented into different groups of consumers will help Sunita to design her promotional material so that it meets the needs of a specific market segment.
   (c) Individual response. For example:
       Personal selling is a marketing tool which Sunita would use to contact her customers or potential customers in person (face-to-face), by telephone or email. Sales promotions, on the other hand, would not involve contacting customers in person. These types of promotion seek to attract a wide range of customers by offering discounts, special offers and free samples.
       Personal selling would take up a lot of Sunita's time.
       Sales promotions may reach a larger number of potential customers.
       If Sunita has established a loyal customer base, she could send out emails to these customers (personal selling) as there is a good chance they will purchase jewellery from the new product range. They may even write positive reviews on social media which Sunita can then use in a follow-up sales promotion campaign.
       In my view, sales promotion is the best way to grow the business and try to reach out to as many new and potential

customers as possible. For a business to grow, it needs to form new customer bases and grow throughout the market. This is difficult to do using personal selling.

Practice assessment 3
(pages 28–41)

1   (a)   D: Statement of account
    (b)   1: Delivery note; 2: Receipt; 3: Credit note
    (c)   (i)   Discount: 5% of £1331.25 = £66.56
          (ii)   VAT is calculated on the total value of the order after the discount: £1331.25 – £66.56 = £1264.69; VAT is 20% of £1264.69 = £252.94
          (iii) Total payable: £1264.69 + £252.94 = £1517.63
    (d)   One from:
          • The customer may not have a bank account.
          • The customer may not have access to technology.
    (e)   To boost sales

2   (a)

Error item	Original amount	Corrected amount
Streamers	£271.50	£281.25
Subtotal	£328.45	£331.25
VAT	£67.75	£66.25

    (b)   One from:
          • To calculate costs, revenue, profit or loss
          • To provide information for financial statements
          • To track payments and orders
          • To calculate how much tax is owed to the government
          • To aid decision-making
          • To monitor business performance
    (c)   Individual response. For example:
          1: Cash; 2: Inventory (stock)
    (d)   Individual response. For example:
          1   The information contained in the statement of financial position can be used to calculate the business's net current assets (working capital). Ashley may need a bank overdraft if his business cannot meet its short-term liabilities.
          2   The statement of financial position provides information on a business's long-term liabilities such as business loans. If the value of a business's long-term liabilities is high, the bank may not be willing to lend him any more money.

3   (a)   (i)   £1750 – £1150 = £600
          (ii)   £1150 – £860 = £290
    (b)   One from:
          • Ashley could have reduced the cost of sales by negotiating discounts with suppliers or switching suppliers.
          • Ashley could have reduced business expenses so there is less money to take away from gross profit.
    (c)   (i)   £11 000 – (£6000 + £1500) = £11 000 – £7500 = £3500
          (ii)   £3000 – £2000 = £1000
          (iii) current assets – current liabilities = (£6000 + £1500) – £2000 = £5500
    (d)   (i)   current ratio $= \dfrac{7500}{2000} = 3.75:1$
          (ii)   liquid capital ratio $= \dfrac{7500 - 6000}{2000} = \dfrac{1500}{2000} = 0.75:1$
    (e)   Individual response. For example:
          The business does not have sufficient cash reserves to meet its current (short-term) liabilities.

4   (a)   (i)   £3200 + £100 = £3300
          (ii)   £2550 – £3350 = –£800
          (iii) £3400 – 200 = £3200
          (iv)   £4240 – £3450 = £790
    (b)   £3250

(c)   The shaded area represents the losses made by the business before it reaches the break-even point, after which profits will be generated. Losses will therefore be generated on all ticket sales up to 400 tickets.
(d)   (i)   The break-even point would increase because he would have to sell more tickets to cover his costs.
      (ii)   Fixed costs would fall, leading to a fall in total costs. The break-even point would fall as fewer tickets would need to be sold to cover costs.

5   (a)   (i)   £700 – £250 = £450
          (ii)   £7125 – £1875 – £2000 = £3250
          (iii) £10 750 – 9795 = £955
    (b)   Individual response. For example:
          Ashley has produced a cash flow forecast so that he can monitor the inflow and outflow of cash and plan for when cash outflows are forecast to exceed cash inflows.
    (c)   The business is forecasting that its cash inflow will be greater than cash outflows in all three months. This means that Ashley will not have to take steps to address any cash shortfalls.
    (d)   One from:
          • He may have to sell the inventory at a lower price than he paid for the inventory, resulting in a financial loss.
          • He may have insufficient inventory to meet customer requirements, resulting in a loss of orders.

6   (a)   Individual response. For example:
          1   Print (e.g. newspapers, leaflets). These are likely to be seen by large numbers of people, either in specific locations or over a wide geographical area. This means that the business is reaching out to customers who are not located in the immediate vicinity, which potentially opens up a much larger customer base for the business.
          2   Ambient (e.g. public places such as shopping centres and bus stops). Outdoor advertising aims to catch the attention of passers-by, and this should benefit the business as it would be targeting lots of potential customers in the local area where Ashley's business is situated.
    (b)   Brand image is a set of beliefs and opinions associated in the minds of consumers with a product, service or enterprise. It is important for Ashley's customers to perceive these beliefs and opinions as positive and as mirroring their own, so that they are more likely to purchase the service from his business.
    (c)   Individual response. For example:
          Markets can be divided into different segments, with each segment made up of consumers with shared characteristics, needs and interests. It is important for Ashley to understand the make-up of his target market so that he can analyse the needs of his customers, develop his services to suit the needs of different market segments and choose promotional methods best suited to the target market for his service.
          Understanding the characteristics of a specific market segment will benefit Ashley's business as it means that he won't waste money on promotional activities that won't reach consumers in his target market. It also means that he can price his products and services in line with the income levels of his target consumers.
          However, a drawback is that obtaining information on his target market will involve undertaking market research and analysis, which takes time and money. This should be considered against the benefits which will arise if his research results in additional sales revenue from his promotional activities.

Practice assessment 4

(pages 42–55)

1   (a)   C: Statement of comprehensive income
    (b)   1: Purchase order; 2: Invoice
    (c)   Two from:
    - Cost of individual items supplied
    - Total cost of goods supplied
    - VAT
    - Postage and packaging
    - Discounts
    (d)   A proof of purchase is needed if the goods have to be returned to the supplier.
    (e)   One from:
    - The *Eazicut* is a low-cost tool, so it is affordable for self-employed electricians.
    - Using the *Eazicut* reduces the time it takes to install electrical connections. This could enable electricians to take on more contracts, resulting in increased revenue.

2   (a)   (i)   £25.95 × 3 = £77.85
            (ii)   £77.85 × 0.2 = £15.57
            (iii)   £77.85 + 15.57 = £93.42
    (b)   The sum of money owed can be set against another purchase from *Eazicut Sales*.
    (c)   The level of sales revenue (turnover) will be under– or overstated.
    (d)   Individual response. For example:
            (i)   Advantage: Jarek's customers can 'buy now and pay later'. This might help with their cash flow.
            (ii)   Disadvantage: Jarek has to pay a fee to the credit card company for each transaction. This will add to his cost of sales.
    (e)   One from:
    - He will have access to a bigger market, which could mean the potential for additional sales.
    - His profits may increase as a result of increased sales, so he will have more money to invest in the business.

3   (a)   (i)   £55 250 (sales) – £31 500 (cost of sales) = £23 750 (gross profit)
            (ii)   £23 750 (gross profit) – £13 375 (total expenses) = £10 375 (net profit)
    (b)   (i)   Gross profit margin $= \frac{23\,750}{55\,250} \times 100 = 42.99\%$

            (ii)   Net profit margin $= \frac{10\,375}{55\,250} \times 100 = 18.78\%$
    (c)   Net profit is calculated by taking the gross profit and subtracting the expenses, whereas the net profit margin is the amount of net profit generated by each sale, usually expressed as a percentage.
    (d)   One from:
    - *Sparks & Cables* might have negotiated discounts with suppliers, thereby reducing its cost of sales.
    - *Sparks & Cables* might have better control of its business expenses.
    (e)   A cash sale results in immediate payment, whereas a credit sale will be paid at a later date.

4   (a)   Fixed cost: rent of the warehouse
            Variable cost: metal sheets (or other materials used to produce the *Eazicut*)
    (b)   Break-even point at £8 $= \frac{£2250}{£8 - £3.50} = \frac{2250}{£4.50} = 500$ units
    (c)   500 × £8 = £4000
    (d)   Break-even point at £6 $= \frac{£2250}{£6 - £3.50} = \frac{£2250}{£2.50} = 900$ units

            Additional number of *Eazicut Junior* sales needed to break even = 900 – 500 = 400 units

    (e)   (i)   £4000
            (ii)   500
            (iii)   700
    (f)   Individual response. For example:
            Break-even analysis is based on a number of assumptions. For example, it assumes that fixed and variable costs remain the same. However, in practice, costs may change. For example, workers may work overtime to produce additional units or receive an increase in their hourly rate of pay, leading to higher variable costs.

5   (a)   (i)   Total inflows should be £3650
            (ii)   Net cash flow should be –£1500
            (iii)   Closing balance should be £500

Item	January £
Eazicut sales	3250
Eazicut Junior sales	400
Total Inflows	**3650**
Salary	1500
Purchase of metal sheeting	2500
Other costs	1150
Total outflow	**5150**
Net cash flow	**–1500**
Opening balance	2000
Closing balance	**500**

    (b)   A cash flow statement is a record of the business's **actual** cash inflows and outflows over a specific period of time, whereas a cash flow forecast is a **prediction** of cash inflows and outflows in the future.
    (c)   One from:
    - Sell assets
    - Hire out assets to another business
    - Put cash into an interest-bearing account
    - Rent out business premises
    - Invest money in another enterprise to gain a share of its profits
    (d)   Individual response. For example:
            1   One advantage is the convenience of online purchases. Online customers can purchase from and pay the business 24 hours a day, 7 days a week.
            2   Online payment services can be directly linked to the customer's bank account. This means they can keep a check on their personal finances.

6   (a)   1   The costs of the promotion and the impact on profit margins need to be considered, because a successful promotion is one in which the increase in sales covers the costs of the promotion.
            2   Some promotion methods are more cost-effective than others. Public relations activities in the form of press releases can place information about the business in the media without paying for the airtime or media space directly.
    (b)   Individual responses. For example:
            Direct marketing happens when an enterprise communicates with a customer directly to try to sell them something, either by phone or via written communication. Direct marketing will enable Jarek to set up an individual relationship with his customers, as he will be able to tailor the message being sent to the customer to meet their needs.

Methods of direct marketing include mail order catalogues, direct mail (junk mail), telemarketing, email marketing and magazines.

The benefit of direct marketing is that it can build positive associations with a brand, leading to repeat sales, and it may also introduce new customers to products. The disadvantages are that uninvited phone calls to consumers may be unwelcome and customers may ignore written communications (especially junk mail and emails).

Additionally, as this is a new product in a new market, Jarek may not have the addresses, phone numbers and email details of customers. He should have invested in market research in order to identify the likely success of the product in his target market.

In conclusion, it might be beneficial to the business to use a range of marketing methods when launching a new product to a different clientele. The existing customers on the *Sparks & Cables* database will be trade customers rather than members of the general public.